Awesome
Hands-on Activities for Teaching
Grammar

BY SUSAN VAN ZILE

D1518017

New York • Toronto • London • Auckland • Sydney
Mexico City • New Delhi • Hong Kong • Buenos Aires

SCHOLASTIC
Teaching
Resources

Acknowledgments

To the Great Creator who generously and lovingly
bestows upon us all that we are and all that we have.

To my magnificent students who inspire me, teach me, and bring
me great joy. Thank you for sharing your gifts and talents.

To my husband Phil, my children Caroline and Taylor,
and my parents for their abiding love, support,
understanding, and encouragement.

To the administration, teachers, and students of the Cumberland
Valley School District who have consistently provided me with a
rich and rewarding academic environment in which to grow.

To Virginia Dooley and Terry Cooper for
making my dreams come true.

To Scholastic for supporting and nurturing children.

Cover design by Josué Castilleja
Interior design by Maria Lilja

ISBN 0-439-43460-2
Copyright © 2003 by Susan Van Zile. All rights reserved.
Printed in the U.S.A.
7 8 9 10   40   10 09 08 07

Contents

Forget Fragments and Rule Out Run-ons

Bibliography and Web Resources

Introduction

The moment I even whisper the word *grammar*, sounds of moaning and groaning reverberate through the classroom. When I ask students why they hate grammar, they invariably reply, "Worksheets!" While I firmly believe some worksheets are absolutely necessary for reinforcement and retention, I have discovered that my students learn best when they engage in hands-on activities that encourage them to discover, inquire, think, and problem-solve. Challenged by students' negative attitudes toward grammar, I decided to research, develop, and experiment with new methodologies to teach grammatical concepts. In this book I share the successful results of my action research. There are mini-lessons, models, reproducibles, rubrics, photographs, and examples of student work to make the strategies easy to implement. My sincere hope is that the lessons and activities presented here challenge and motivate students and create an environment that promotes inquiry and enthusiasm.

Motivation In his book *Powerful Learning*, Ron Brandt states, "People learn what is personally meaningful to them" (Brandt, 1998, p. 5). To make grammar meaningful to students and to motivate them, Brandt and other researchers believe educators must discover engaging ways to approach the required content and employ creative teaching and learning practices. "Intrinsic motivation is stimulated by tasks of optimal novelty and difficulty" (Brandt, 1998, p. 6).

Because I believe that deep understanding occurs when students make connections, I do not use these activities and strategies in isolation. Instead, I integrate grammar instruction with reading, writing, speaking, and listening skills. Furthermore, I often teach grammar in conjunction with thematic units. For example, my theme for nouns is friendship. Students read and discuss stories about friendship and write about their personal experiences with friendship. The context of the stories and students' writing then forms the foundation for teaching nouns. For instance, my learning center for identifying nouns is a composition about best friends. To be exceptionally effective learning tools, the hands-on activities in this book should be used within the context of an integrated unit. The concepts presented also need to be reinforced through practice and retention exercises.

Although I have experienced failures as well as successes in my hands-on approach to teaching, the results are definitely worth the time and energy devoted to preparation. Each time I design a lesson, I ask myself, "How can I make learning more meaningful for my students? How can I help them think and create?" Not long ago, my lessons on possessive nouns looked far different from the way they look today. In fact, I dreaded the word *possessive* because it confused, befuddled, and bored my students. Since I started my journey into creating powerful, hands-on learning, both my students and I have benefited. Now they enjoy punctuating possessives, and I love teaching them. As the class proudly and enthusiastically presents their *Perfectly Punctuated Possessive Plays*, I beam, laugh, and loudly applaud. With open arms my students and I welcome and celebrate new knowledge each day. This is my dream for all of us; may we forever dance in the light of learning.

Nifty Nouns

The activities in this chapter are designed to promote brain-compatible learning. According to brain research, instruction should reflect four major principles: comfort, challenge, choice, and connections. To activate students' prior knowledge about nouns, the pantomine activity uses movement and categorization to discover what students already know. The noun nature poems, possessive plays, learning centers, and multiple intelligences activities generate enthusiasm, provide choice, and build specific, learner-controlled feedback into each challenge. These novel, stimulating activities not only promote learning but also create a joyful classroom environment.

Brain Research and Learning "The key to getting smarter is making more connections between brain cells and not losing existing connections" (Jensen, 1998, p. 15). To forge these connections, link new knowledge to prior knowledge, engage emotions, encourage social interaction, and create hands-on, experiential activities that help students seek patterns.

Activity 1 — Noun Pantomimes

Objectives	To activate students' prior knowledge about nouns with a bodily-kinesthetic game; to identify and categorize nouns
Time	One 40-minute class period
Materials	● index cards (one per student) with different nouns written on them (include a variety of persons, places, things, and ideas) ● notebook paper ● pencils ● chalk

Step-by-Step

1. Tell students that they are going to play a game designed to teach them about a concept. (Do not use the word *noun* when introducing the activity.)

2. Place an index card with a noun written on it facedown on each student's desk. After all students receive a card, instruct them to look at the word. Remind them not to share the word with anyone.

3. Explain to students that they are to use gestures, not speech, to physically demonstrate the noun on their cards. Model one or two examples for students. For example, to show the noun *rabbit*, you can hop and wiggle your nose.

4. Call one student at a time to the front of the room to act out his or her noun. Allow students about one minute to convey the word to the class. If the class has not guessed the word,

the student actor tells the class the word. (Coach students who ask for ideas about how to act out their word.)

5. When the correct response is given, write the word on the board, and have all of the students record the word on notebook paper.

6. After students guess all of the words and discover what they have in common, ask them to categorize the nouns on their notebook paper using the following abbreviations:

   PR = person; PL = place; T = thing; I = idea.

7. Review and discuss the correct answers with students.

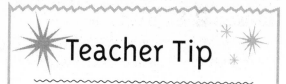

Teacher Tip

Expand the noun categories for older students. Include examples of common, proper, abstract, concrete, collective, singular, and plural nouns on the index cards. Then have students work in groups or with a partner to determine which categories fit each word.

Activity 2 ## Noun Nature Poems

Lesson 1: General vs. Specific Nouns

Objectives	To introduce the concept of specific, exact, or precise nouns; to list specific nature nouns
Time	One 40-minute class period
Materials	● paper (1 piece per student) ● pencils (1 per student) ● coats or appropriate outerwear

Step-by-Step

1. Write a general noun, such as *tree*, *cat*, or *car*, on the board. Ask students to provide more exact or specific word choices for these nouns. For example, instead of *tree*, substitute *oak* or *birch*. Record students' choices on the board.

2. Once students understand the concept of a specific noun, explain that they are going on a nature walk to collect nouns, which they will use to create nature poems. Have students work with partners to collectively brainstorm as many precise nouns as possible while they walk.

3. After the walk, have student pairs share their lists with each other. During this time, have students eliminate the general nouns recorded and add new specific nouns that were not on their lists.

Lesson 2: Similes

Objectives	To introduce and generate original similes; to create nature poems using similes and exact nouns
Time	One 40-minute class period
Materials	❀ an overhead transparency of unfinished similes
	❀ an overhead transparency of the noun nature poem models (page 24)

Step-by-Step

1. Introduce similes. On the board, write and underline the following three nature similes from Eve Merriam's poem *Willow and Gingko*:

   "The willow's branches are <u>like silken thread</u>."

   "The willow is sleek <u>as a velvet-nosed calf</u>."

   "The willow's music is <u>like a soprano</u>, Delicate and thin."

2. Ask students what they observe about the underlined phrases. Elicit the definition of a simile from students and discuss the comparisons Merriam makes.

3. Have students picture themselves embracing or climbing the trunk of a favorite or familiar tree. Ask what the tree feels like (gnarled knuckles on an old man's hands; Dad's unshaven whiskers) or looks like (a moss-covered statue; an ancient Greek column).

4. Then show the following nature similes on an overhead transparency and ask students to complete them. Encourage students to create original similes instead of using more common expressions such as "red as a rose" or "shiny like a diamond."

The lily-covered lake looks like _____.

Flocks of cardinals chattered like _____.

The fresh, falling snow feels like _____.

White pines smell like _____.

Crisp leaves crunch as loudly as _____.

Grandma's Apple Tree

My gorgeous leaves sway like the calm rocking of a swing.
My delicious apples taste like sweet spring water.
Brilliant buds glow like a warm winter fire.
White blossoms drop like a gentle snowfall.
My smooth bark feels like silky velvet.
My delicate branches spread like dew on the morning grass.
I bud; I blossom; I grow my fruit.
My leaves then fall as I go to sleep.

5. Explain to students that they are going to use similes as well as the exact nouns from their nature walks to create an original poem. After they choose an object in nature, they may write a description of it, or they may write a poem from its point of view. Require the poem to contain a minimum of five underlined exact nouns and two similes. To help students understand the assignment, on the overhead projector, show the two versions of "The Majestic Birch" as models.

6. Be sure students follow the steps of the writing process, including drafting, peer conferencing, editing, revision, and publication. Ask students to illustrate their poems, then display their final products.

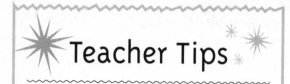

Teacher Tips

To help students use precise nouns to identify objects in nature, I provide field guides to plants, birds, and trees and ask our school librarian to reserve other sources that will assist students in their quest for nature nouns.

If your school is located in an urban setting, direct students to observe the plants, flowers, trees, and animals in the vicinity. If possible, take them to a local park.

Activity 3 # Patterns of Plurals

Objectives	To develop students' thinking skills and to encourage them to discover the rules and patterns for forming plurals; to discover and write the rules for forming the plurals of nouns
Time	One or two 40-minute class periods
Materials	◉ envelopes (one per pair of students) containing one laminated set of cards with patterns of plurals word pairs (page 11) ◉ overhead projector markers
	◉ spray bottles filled with water ◉ paper towels
	◉ paper for recording the rules for forming plurals

Step-by-Step

1. Before class, prepare laminated sets of Patterns of Plurals cards using the suggested word pairs on the next page. Put each set of cards into a separate envelope.

2. Distribute one envelope, a transparency marker, and clean-up materials to each pair of students.

3. Ask partners to spread the cards on their desks and look for patterns among the singular and plural word endings. Provide the following directions:

• Examine the word endings for both the singular and plural nouns.

• Group together the words that have similar patterns in their endings. Use the overhead transparency pen to circle the patterns.

4. Circulate through the room and ask students questions that lead them to discover the patterns.

5. Ask students to share all of their categories and the related words. Then have students state the rule for forming plurals of nouns that the pattern illustrates. Write the rule and the words that exemplify it on the board. Have students record the examples and rules on a piece of notebook paper titled "Rules for Forming Plurals of Nouns." Refer to the sample rules below.

Suggested Patterns of Plurals Word Pairs

pencil—pencils
teacher—teachers
clock—clocks
gas—gases
glass—glasses
brush—brushes
church—churches
box—boxes

buzz—buzzes
tomato—tomatoes
potato—potatoes
hero—heroes
echo—echoes
piano—pianos
taco—tacos
baby—babies

country—countries
lady—ladies
key—keys
turkey—turkeys
donkey—donkeys
chief—chiefs
roof—roofs
wolf—wolves

leaf—leaves
life—lives
knife—knives
deer—deer
sheep—sheep
child—children
goose—geese
man—men

Rules for Forming Plurals of Nouns

A. Add "s" to form the plurals of most singular nouns:
    pencil—pencils; teacher—teachers; clock—clocks

B. When the singular noun ends in s, ss, sh, ch, x, or z, add "es": gas—gases; glass—glasses; brush—brushes; church—churches; box—boxes; buzz—buzzes

C. When the singular noun ends in o, add "s" (exceptions: tomatoes, potatoes, heroes, echoes): piano—pianos; taco—tacos

D. When the singular noun ends with a consonant + y, change the y to i and add "es": baby—babies; country—countries; lady—ladies

E. When the singular noun ends with a vowel + y, just add "s": key—keys; turkey—turkeys; donkey—donkeys

F. For most singular nouns ending in f or fe, add "s." For some nouns ending in f or fe, change the f to v and "es" or "s": chief—chiefs; roof—roofs; wolf—wolves; leaf—leaves; life—lives; knife—knives

G. Some nouns stay the same whether they are singular or plural: deer—deer; sheep—sheep

H. Some singular nouns form their plurals in special ways: child—children; goose—geese; man—men

Perfectly Punctuated Possessive Plays

Lesson 1: Introducing Possessive Nouns

Objectives	To understand the meaning of possessive nouns; to correctly use the apostrophe to show possession; to get the information into students' long-term memories; to incorporate fast-paced reinforcement activities that require students to move
Time	One 40-minute class period
Materials	● laminated 12" x 18" cards (one per student) containing examples of singular, plural, and irregular possessives (page 13)
	● three laminated 12" x 18" cards stating the rules for forming possessives (page 13)

Step-by-Step

1. Before class, prepare the possessive noun cards and laminated rule cards. Place a card facedown on each student's desk. Post the laminated rule cards in different sections of the classroom.

2. Ask students to turn over the card on their desk and study it. Tell them to move around, organizing themselves into three different groups (singular, plural, and irregular). Prompt them to discover the similarities and differences for forming possessives.

3. Then have students go to whatever section of the room relates to the card they're holding. Start with the singular possessive group. Point to each student, and have him or her cover the apostrophe. Ask the class to tell you whether the noun is singular or plural. Then use the word in a sentence and write the sentence on the board.

4. Ask students to state the rule for forming singular possessives. Then have them add movement as they state the rule. When they say, "Add an apostrophe," have them raise one hand and draw the apostrophe in the air. As they say *s*, have them move their bodies in the shape of an s (a wiggle). Practice several times and then have each student with a singular possessive card hold it up while the rest of the class acts out the rule.

5. Teach the other two rules in the same way, switching the order for the plural possessive. Remember to set a lively pace to keep students motivated and moving.

Rules for Forming Possessives

To form the possessive of a singular noun, add an apostrophe (') first and then add the s. Examples: a man's briefcase; one girl's shirt

To form the possessive of a plural noun ending in s, add an apostrophe (') after the s. Examples: several boys' footballs; the Lewises' cars

To form the possessive of an irregular plural noun that does not end in s, add an apostrophe (') and then add the s. Examples: the women's hats; the children's toys

Teacher Tip

Adjust instruction to meet the needs of your class. Upper-level students may only need to review five of the possessive noun cards to activate prior knowledge of possessive nouns. Younger students may need to proceed more slowly. Because the goal of the activity is to have students begin to internalize the rules for forming possessive nouns, repetition and reinforcement of those rules is essential.

Because the cerebellum processes both movement and learning, movement is vital to cognition. Consequently, when introducing possessive nouns to students, use physical gestures. You can "invent procedures, so that students will, through repetition, place subject matter into procedural memory. Try anything that provides movement" (Sprenger, 1999, p. 75).

Lesson 2: Noun Skits

Objectives	To correctly use and punctuate possessive nouns in writing; to use speaking, listening, and performing skills to present possessive noun skits
Time	One or two 40-minute class periods
Materials	● paper lunch bags (one for each group of four students) containing four sets of novel objects, such as animal noses, maracas, and yo-yos
	● colored markers (one for each student)
	● 12" x 18" white construction paper (one sheet for each student)
	● four 12" x 18" laminated cards containing the lines of the model script
	● props for the model skit

Step-by-Step

1. Using a yo-yo, model a possessive noun skit (page 15). The script includes separate sentences for each of these noun types: singular possessive, plural noun, plural possessive, and irregular plural possessive. Before beginning the skit, coach student volunteers to not wind the yo-yo string too tightly. Encourage them to make humorous gestures and facial expressions to create a slapstick comedy effect.

2. After presenting the model, divide students into groups of four. Distribute the construction paper, markers, and paper bag with objects to each group, but do not allow them to open the bags.

3. Explain to the groups that they will use the objects in the bags to write a short possessive noun skit similar to the model that includes one singular possessive, one plural noun, one plural possessive, and one irregular plural possessive.

4. Allow time for students to write, practice, and perform the skits. Circulate to monitor student progress as they work.

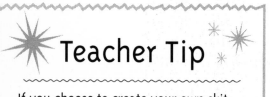

Teacher Tip

If you choose to create your own skit, you may also want to model your writing process for students.

CARD 1

Singular Possessive

Help! The <u>yo-yo's</u> string is caught around my ankle!

(A student winds yo-yo string around the teacher's ankle.)

CARD 2

Plural Noun

Oh no! The <u>yo-yos</u> are attacking me!

(Two students wind string from two yo-yos around the teacher's ankles.)

CARD 3

Plural Possessive

The <u>yo-yos'</u> strings have trapped me!

(The teacher tries frantically to escape from the mess of strings.)

CARD 4

Irregular Plural Possessive

They sure don't make <u>children's</u> toys the way they used to.

(The teacher looks chagrined, staring at the mess of yo-yo string wound around her ankles.)

Because possessives are difficult for most students, the novel objects used in the plays —such as big nose disguises, yo-yos, and maracas—motivate students to learn.

Differentiating Instruction With Noun Learning Centers

Objective	To provide various options for learning information about nouns
Time	Two centers or one multiple-intelligences project per 40-minute class period
Materials	● center-specific step-by-step directions and answer keys for self-correction

Step-by-Step

1. Create a set of directions, a materials list, and an answer key for each center (use the computer and large fonts, and print on legal-size paper). Then laminate them.

2. Gather the needed reproducible pages. Enlarge these to poster size, as necessary, and laminate.

3. Briefly introduce students to each center.

4. Review your general rules for Learning Centers and any other student requirements you may have. (See page 17 for some of my rules.)

5. Move around the room monitoring students. If students demonstrate mastery of nouns, allow them to design a related independent project.

6. For centers that require using overhead projector markers, always provide plenty of paper towels and a spray bottle filled with water for cleaning up. Remind students not to squirt laminated posters or cards directly. Instead, they should wet a paper towel and then use it to wipe off the ink.

"Individuals learn differently" (Brandt, 1998, p. 7). Therefore, teachers need to offer students choices about how and what they learn. Differentiating instruction means "shaking up what goes on inside the classroom so that students have multiple options for taking in information, making sense of ideas, and expressing what they learn" (Tomlinson, 1995, p. 3).

Center 1: Identifying Nouns

Objective   Using an overhead projector marker, students identify nouns in a poster-size, first-person narrative about a friendship between a young person and Gerald the Gila monster.

Materials
- Best Friends (page 25)
- overhead projector markers
- answer key
- clean-up materials

Student Directions

1. Using an overhead projector marker, circle the nouns in "Best Friends." If you are working in teams or partners, take turns identifying the nouns.
2. Check your work. Use the answer key and make any needed corrections.
3. Clean up the materials.

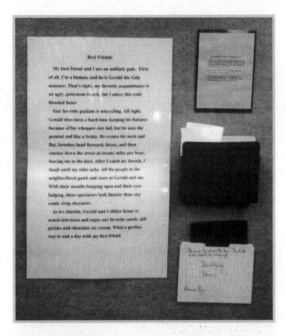

Answer Key

PARAGRAPH 1 friend, pair, human, Gerald, Gila monster, acquaintance, lizard, beast

PARAGRAPH 2 pastime, unicycling, Gerald, time, balance, tail, end, brake, neck, head, street, miles, hour, dust, breath, sides, people, neighborhood, Gerald, mouths, eyes, spectators, character

PARAGRAPH 3 Gerald, home, television, snack, dill pickles (or just pickles), ice cream, way, day, friend

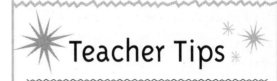

Teacher Tips

Some of My Learning Center Rules

1. Up to four students in a center.
2. Speak in "six-inch" voices.
3. Share materials and take turns.
4. Read all directions for the center first.
5. Clean materials and return them to the appropriate area.

I store the materials for each center—including spray bottles, overhead transparency markers, and answer keys—in expandable pocket folders. I also use large manila envelopes to house card games and small manipulatives. I place markers, scissors, construction paper, glue sticks, rulers, and other materials students may need to complete the multiple-intelligences centers on a table or a counter in the room.

Center 2: Common or Proper?

Objective   Students match a common noun to the appropriate proper noun. (To make the activity more challenging, the proper nouns are not capitalized.)

Materials   🌼 Common or Proper? cards (page 26)
                  🌼 overhead projector markers
                  🌼 clean-up materials

Student Directions

1. Match a common noun to the appropriate proper noun.
2. Using an overhead projector marker, edit the nouns for capitalization.
3. Check your work. Use the answer key and make any needed corrections.
4. Clean up the materials.

Center Tips   🌼 To create an answer key, copy the reproducible and use proofreading symbols to capitalize the proper nouns.

| mars | | planet |

🌼 Create extra common and proper noun combinations, as necessary.

Awesome Hands-on Activities for Teaching Grammar

Center 3: Make It Plural

Objective In sentences about friendship, students fill in the blanks with plural forms of nouns and identify the rule that tells how the plural was formed.

Materials
- Rules for Forming Plurals of Nouns (page 11)
- Friendship Sentences (page 27)
- overhead transparency markers
- answer key
- clean-up materials

Student Directions

1. Using the Rules for Forming Plurals of Nouns as a reference, fill in the blanks on the Friendship Sentences sheet with an overhead projector marker.
2. When you have finished filling in the examples, create your own friendship sentences for a classmate to fill in.
3. Check your work. Make any needed corrections.
4. Clean up the materials.

Answer Key

1. D; diaries 2. B; watches 3. C; heroes
4. D; cities 5. F; leaves

Example

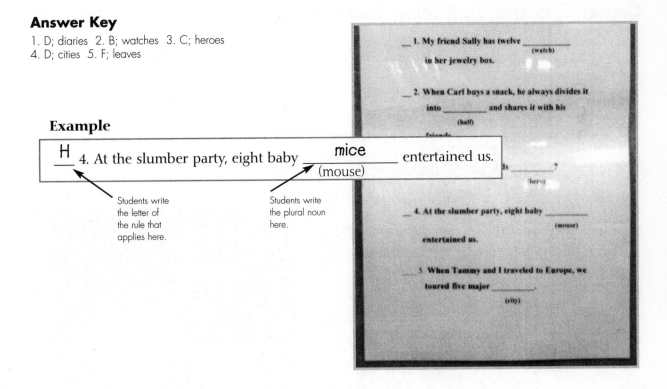

__H__ 4. At the slumber party, eight baby ___mice___ entertained us.
(mouse)

Students write the letter of the rule that applies here.

Students write the plural noun here.

Center 4: Be Aggressive and Learn Your Possessives

Objective   Two or three students play a card game that reinforces the correct use of possessives.

Materials
- Be Aggressive and Learn Your Possessives cards (pages 28 and 29)
- one to two dry erase boards
- one to two dry erase markers
- clean-up materials

Student Directions

1. Place the cards in a pile facedown and take turns drawing a card.
2. The person who draws the card reads it to the other players.
3. Write the possessive form of the noun that is read to you on the white board with the special pen. You may need to make the noun plural first.
4. Have the reader check your answers. The player with the most correct answers wins.
5. Clean the white boards.

Center 5: Nouns That Show Possession

Objective   On a poster-sized list of singular, plural, and irregular plural nouns, students use hook-and-loop fastened *apostrophe* and *s* cards to form possessive nouns.

Materials
- Nouns That Show Possession (page 30)
- envelope containing apostrophes and *s*'s (page 31) with the rough side of a hook-and-loop fastener on the back
- answer key
- clean-up materials

Student Directions

Using the materials in the envelope, form the possessive of each of the nouns.

Center Tip   At the end of each noun on the poster, place two pieces of hook-and-loop fasteners (use the soft side). This will prevent students from automatically knowing the answers.

Example: students ■ ■ books

hook-and-loop fasteners

Answer Key

1. students' books 2. Bess's dress 3. children's games 4. neighbors' lawns 5. owl's wings 6. brother's hula hoop
7. babies' bottles 8. Joneses' hamsters 9. sheep's wool 10. actress's script

Awesome Hands-on Activities for Teaching Grammar

Center 6: Categorizing Plurals and Possessives

Objective   Students determine whether an underlined noun in a phrase is a plural, singular possessive, or plural possessive noun and attach the phrase in the appropriate category on a large chart.

Materials
- Categorizing Plurals and Possessives (page 32)
- envelope containing plural, singular possessive, and plural possessive noun phrases (page 33) with the rough side of a hook-and-loop fastener on the back
- answer key
- clean-up materials

Student Directions

See page 32.

Center Tips
- Put a piece of hook-and-loop fastener (use the soft side) in the center of each row on the chart.
- Create extra plural and possessive cards, as necessary.

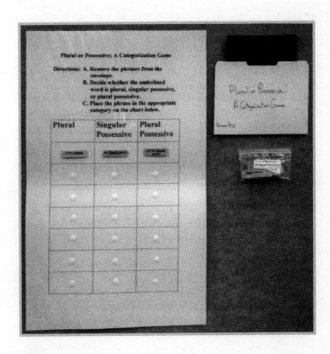

Teacher Observation

When I asked the learning support teacher why the Noun Centers improved student achievement on the noun test, she replied, "The movement, especially the cover-up strategy and the Velcro® centers really benefited my kids. I believe the tactile manipulation of the Velcro® helped them distinguish the differences among the various types of possessives. I also noticed as students moved around the centers, they interacted with one another and explained their answers."

Answer Key

Plural: six <u>lives</u>, three <u>toys</u>, a few <u>friends</u>, a couple of <u>waitresses</u>, several <u>Chrises</u>, broken <u>glasses</u>, numerous paint <u>brushes</u>

Singular Possessive: <u>life's</u> journey, my <u>friend's</u> party, the <u>waitress's</u> tray, a <u>toy's</u> box, <u>Chris's</u> phone, a <u>glass's</u> rim, the <u>brush's</u> handle

Plural Possessive: several <u>friends'</u> movies, many <u>toys'</u> wheels, ten <u>waitresses'</u> uniforms, the <u>Davises'</u> cars

Center 7: Specific or Exact Nouns

Objective
Students use laminated word wheels to generate a minimum of six specific nouns for the general noun found in the center of the wheel.

Materials
🌀 five laminated word wheels with general nouns written in the center
🌀 overhead transparency markers

Center Tip
Try some of these general nouns:
- animal
- fruit
- building
- music

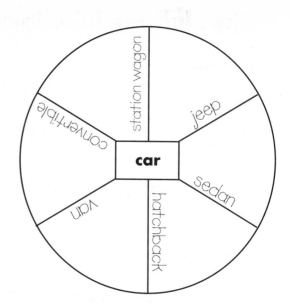

Center 8: Abstract or Concrete?

Objective
Students categorize concrete and abstract nouns.

Materials
🌀 set of 20 cards containing abstract and concrete nouns
🌀 two category cards labeled *Abstract* and *Concrete*

Center Tip
Try some of these abstract and concrete nouns:
- peace
- love
- hope
- sadness
- wisdom
- friend
- heart
- smile
- frown
- book

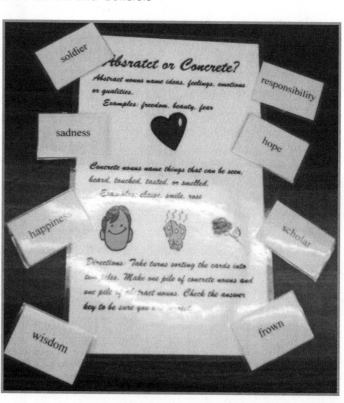

Awesome Hands-on Activities for Teaching Grammar

The Multiple Intelligences Centers

Objective   Students experience four of the eight multiple intelligences (the other noun centers and activities address the rest of them)

Materials   These centers are simply colorful posters that contain the student directions for the activity.

Center 9: Interpersonal Nouns

With a partner, interview a noun. One student is a famous interviewer, such as Oprah Winfrey, and the other is the noun.

Center 10: Intrapersonal Nouns

Write a paragraph describing yourself, your hobbies, interests, likes, and dislikes. Include the following noun types, which you underline and label: two common, two proper, one singular, one plural, one singular possessive, one plural possessive, and one irregular possessive.

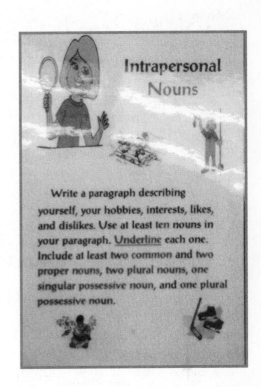

Center 11: Musical Rhythmic Nouns

Create a song, rap, or jingle about nouns. In the song, include information about common, proper, singular, plural, and possessive nouns.

Center 12: Visual Spatial Nouns

Design a noun pictograph—a story that uses both words and pictures. Instead of using nouns in the story, draw pictures representing the nouns.

The Majestic Birch

(a description of the object)

The leafless <u>birch</u> dances like soft, wispy <u>willows</u>.

This joyful <u>ballerina</u> flutters like a jeweled <u>hummingbird's</u> wings.

Its delicate <u>branches</u> sweep skyward like praying hands.

Minuscule <u>buds</u> hide like hermit <u>crabs</u> deep inside their shells.

Brittle <u>bark</u> shreds and sheds like <u>strands</u> of silky hair.

Supple <u>limbs</u> wind and twist like mountainous country roads.

The resplendent birch stretches toward the light.

The Majestic Birch

(written from the object's point of view)

Frigid winds chill my barren <u>branches</u>.

I shudder and shake like a <u>toddler</u> relentlessly creating

Snow <u>angels</u> on a snow-covered frozen <u>pond</u>.

How I long for <u>shafts</u> of scorching <u>sunlight</u>

To warm my tender <u>buds</u>

Which slumber inside fragile shells

Like <u>butterflies</u> burrowed in <u>cocoons</u>.

Winter winds, take flight.

Allow me to reveal my emerald finery.

Best Friends

My best friend and I are an unlikely pair. First of all, I'm a human, and he is Gerald the Gila monster. That's right, my favorite acquaintance is an ugly, poisonous lizard, but I adore this cold-blooded beast.

Our favorite pastime is unicycling. All right, Gerald does have a hard time keeping his balance because of his whopper-sized tail, but he uses the pointed end like a brake. He cranes his neck and flat, formless head forward, hisses, and then smokes down the street at twenty miles per hour, leaving me in the dust. After I catch my breath, I laugh until my sides ache. All the people in the neighborhood gawk and stare at Gerald and me. With their mouths hanging open and their eyes bulging, these spectators look funnier than any comic strip character.

As we chuckle, Gerald and I slither home to watch television and enjoy our favorite snack: dill pickles and chocolate ice cream. What a perfect way to end a day with my best friend.

thursday	day
ohio river	river
wyoming	state
white house	building
mars	planet
chicago	city
puerto rico	island
veteran's day	holiday

Friendship Sentences

1. ___ Do your friends ever let you read their _____?
(diary)

2. ___ How many _____ does your sister own?
(watch)

3. ___ Are any of your friends _____?
(hero)

4. ___ When my friend's family traveled to Europe, they toured five major _____ .
(city)

5. ___ My best friend and I always like to rake _____ together in autumn.
(leaf)

Create your own friendship sentences that are missing plural nouns. Remember to include a singular noun as a clue. Then see if a classmate can fill in the blanks.

_____

_____

_____

_____

_____

_____

Write the possessive form of the noun. You may need to make the noun plural first.

1. (friend) My ___ funny bone causes trouble.

Answer: friend's

Write the possessive form of the noun. You may need to make the noun plural first.

2. (bass) On our camping trip, a ___ head appeared in my bed.

Answer: bass's

Write the possessive form of the noun. You may need to make the noun plural first.

3. (weed) For a "flower arrangement," Liz put ___ stems in water.

Answer: weeds'

Write the possessive form of the noun. You may need to make the noun plural first.

4. (tent) Liz laughed when the ___ pole wobbled and then collapsed.

Answer: tent's

Write the possessive form of the noun. You may need to make the noun plural first.

5. (foot) When I was sleeping, Liz painted smiley faces on both of my ___ soles!

Answer: feet's

Write the possessive form of the noun. You may need to make the noun plural first.

6. (man) At the lake, Liz strolled around wearing suspenders and two pairs of ___ pants.

Answer: men's

Write the possessive form of the noun. You may need to make the noun plural first.

7. (lady) In response to Liz's weird outfit, three ___ mouths dropped to their knees!

Answer: ladies'

Write the possessive form of the noun. You may need to make the noun plural first.

8. (Jones) After Liz hollered, "Boo!" from the bushes, six of the ___ faces looked terrified.

Answer: Joneses'

Write the possessive form of the noun. You may need to make the noun plural first.

9. (radio) One of Liz's pranks involved removing several ___ batteries.

Answer: radios'

Write the possessive form of the noun. You may need to make the noun plural first.

10. (person) Angry ___ shouts and complaints about missing batteries echoed through camp like thunder.

Answer: people's

Write the possessive form of the noun. You may need to make the noun plural first.

11. (Bess) Our friend ___ blood was boiling when she discovered a pile of batteries near our tent.

Answer: Bess's

Write the possessive form of the noun. You may need to make the noun plural first.

16. (woman) Liz laughed, climbed the flagpole, and topped it with a ___ wig.

Answer: woman's

Write the possessive form of the noun. You may need to make the noun plural first.

12. (camper) The eight ___ plan for revenge hatched quickly.

Answer: campers'

Write the possessive form of the noun. You may need to make the noun plural first.

17. (child) The ___ group decided to add to the fun.

Answer: children's

Write the possessive form of the noun. You may need to make the noun plural first.

13. (Liz) ___underwear, dyed hot pink, flew from the flagpole in the morning.

Answer: Liz's

Write the possessive form of the noun. You may need to make the noun plural first.

18. (director) They stole the camp ___ toupee and placed it on the flagpole.

Answer: director's

Write the possessive form of the noun. You may need to make the noun plural first.

14. (frog) Awakened by the ___ croaks, Liz suddenly spied familiar-looking underwear.

Answer: frogs'

Write the possessive form of the noun. You may need to make the noun plural first.

19. (fellow) Embarrassed, the ___ humor prevailed, and, bald as a cue, he danced the Irish jig.

Answer: fellow's

Write the possessive form of the noun. You may need to make the noun plural first.

15. (girl) The ___ reaction to the joke surprised us all.

Answer: girl's

Write the possessive form of the noun. You may need to make the noun plural first.

20. (boss) Following the ___ lead, the campers began singing Irish tunes and whirling around the flagpole.

Answer: boss's

1. students__ __ books

2. Bess__ __ dress

3. children__ __ games

4. neighbors__ __ lawns

5. owl__ __ wings

6. brother__ __ hula hoop

7. babies__ __ bottles

8. Joneses__ __ hamsters

9. sheep__ __ wool

10. actress__ __ script

S	S	S	S	S	S	S	,	,	,	,	,	,	,	,
S	S	S	S	S	S	S	,	,	,	,	,	,	,	,
S	S	S	S	S	S	S	,	,	,	,	,	,	,	,
S	S	S	S	S	S	S	,	,	,	,	,	,	,	,
S	S	S	S	S	S	S	,	,	,	,	,	,	,	,
S	S	S	S	S	S	S	,	,	,	,	,	,	,	,
S	S	S	S	S	S	S	,	,	,	,	,	,	,	,
S	S	S	S	S	S	S	,	,	,	,	,	,	,	,
S	S	S	S	S	S	S	,	,	,	,	,	,	,	,
S	S	S	S	S	S	S	,	,	,	,	,	,	,	,
S	S	S	S	S	S	S	,	,	,	,	,	,	,	,
S	S	S	S	S	S	S	,	,	,	,	,	,	,	,

Directions: A. Remove the phrases from the envelope.
                B. Decide whether the underlined word is plural, singular possessive,
                   or plural possessive.
                C. Place the phrase in the appropriate category on the chart below.

Plural	Singular Possessive	Plural Possessive

six <u>lives</u>	several <u>friends'</u> movies	<u>life's</u> journey
my <u>friend's</u> party	three <u>toys</u>	a few <u>friends</u>
many <u>toys'</u> wheels	the <u>waitress's</u> tray	a <u>toy's</u> box
a couple of <u>waitresses</u>	<u>Chris's</u> phone	ten <u>waitresses'</u> uniforms
several <u>Chrises</u>	broken <u>glasses</u>	the <u>Davises'</u> cars
a <u>glass's</u> rim	the <u>brush's</u> handle	numerous paint <u>brushes</u>

Vivid Verbs

Because movement and positive emotions are critical to cognition, the mnemonics presented here use both of these elements to drive learning. One fun-filled strategy teaches students how to sing the helping verbs to the tune of "Jingle Bells."

To help students eliminate what I call "boo hisser" verbs from their compositions, instructions for writing and performing vivid verb cheers are provided. There are also examples of assessment activities designed to integrate students' multiple intelligences and learning styles. In short, the verb strategies in this chapter engage students both physically and emotionally to promote cognition.

> **Emotions, Movement, and Cognition**
>
> "Emotions drive attention, create meaning, and have their own memory pathways" (Jensen, 1998, p. 72). Consequently, activating and engaging positive emotions is critical to cognition; so is movement. The cerebellum, which processes movement, also processes learning. Numerous studies link the cerebellum to "memory, spatial perception, language, attention, nonverbal cues, and even decision-making" (Jensen, 1998, p. 84).

Activity 1 — Movin' and Groovin' With Verbs

Objective	To activate students' prior knowledge of verbs by using a combination of movement and brainstorming
Time	One 40-minute class period
Materials	● index cards containing overused verbs (one per group)

Step-by-Step

1. Ask students to brainstorm words that complete this sentence: "The sleepy, ancient dragon _____ down the road." After you create a grand list of verbs on the board, ask, "What part of speech have you just created?" Students respond, "Verbs."

2. To help define the word *verb*, teach students this chant:

   A verb is something you can do.
   It makes you want to move.
   It makes you want to groo-oo-oove.

   As you chant together, move to the beat, shaking your upper bodies and shoulders forward on the first line and backward on the second. On the word *groo-oo-oove*, do the twist until you are close to the floor. Move and chant several times to perfect the beat and rhythm.

3. Ask students, "Which of the verbs we listed do you think are lively and exciting?" Check off the words students suggest. Inevitably, the verb *walks* appears on the board, which can lead to a discussion of the difference between a tired,

overused verb and a "vivid verb." Emphasize that vivid verbs paint glorious, descriptive pictures in writing.

4. To demonstrate how the different verbs on the board change the meaning of the sentence, have students stand up and physically act out the meanings of words such as *shuffles*, *limps*, *waddles*, and *stumbles*.

5. Give groups of four students an index card containing an overused verb such as *eat*, *look*, *come*, or *run*. Have students brainstorm as many vivid verbs as they can to replace it. Groups should record and share their lists with the class.

6. Collect and type the lists to produce a student-generated vivid verb bank for the class.

Activity 2 | Vivid Verb Cheers

Objectives	To motivate students to use vivid action verbs in their writing by incorporating the verbal-linguistic, musical-rhythmic, and bodily-kinesthetic intelligences into the production of vivid verb cheers; to use five or more vivid verbs in a cheer; to develop writing, speaking, and performing skills by composing and presenting cheers
Time	Two to three 40-minute class periods
Materials	● overhead transparency of the model cheer (page 36) ● copies (one per student) of the Vivid Verb Cheer Rubric (page 43) ● props: stuffed dragon, football, pom-poms (optional) ● video camera and player (optional)

Step-by-Step

1. Divide students into small groups of 2 to 4 and explain that they are going to write and perform cheers that include at least five vivid verbs.

2. Model and physically demonstrate the cheer on the next page or a similar one. Ham it up by using pom-poms, a football, and a stuffed dragon as props. Remember to act out the verbs as well.

3. Next, ask students to select a team name and the sport about which they will write. Students should brainstorm lists of vivid verbs that rhyme and that fit the sport selected. If students choose football, for example, their list might include the following verbs:

crackle, tackle, shackle; bumble, fumble, rumble, stumble, tumble; hike, spike; bash crash, dash, smash

4. After they brainstorm, have students compose their rough drafts. Because the cheers must be memorized, have every group member write.

Teacher Tips

To introduce the vivid verb cheers, I give students a copy of the rubric, which we collectively review. Then I have the class use it to evaluate two cheers I videotaped from the previous year. We critique one good example and one that is not as well done. This activity deepens students' understanding of the project and appears to improve their performance.

Photograph the cheerleaders on performance day. Use the pictures and cheers to create a hall or bulletin board display. Make simple awards to celebrate student successes, such as Most Vivacious Verbs, Most Hilarious, or Awesome Action.

5. Have groups edit the drafts, write legible final copies with the vivid verbs underlined, add illustrations, make a list of props to bring, and practice their performances.

6. Set up a video camera and organize groups for a whole-class performance.

7. Pair groups together and have peers use the Vivid Verb Cheer Rubric to evaluate each other's performance. Then collect the rubrics.

8. The next day, show students the videotape. Ask them to focus on the speaking and performing skills, then discuss their observations. Ask students to write a paragraph describing two things they did well, two things they can improve, and two things they learned from the experience.

Model Vivid Verb Cheer:

The Dragon Slayers

We're the Dragon Slayers.
We <u>chant</u> and <u>cheer</u>
'Cause we're the best
Team of the year.
We <u>tackle</u>, <u>rumble</u>,
Then nail the ball
'Cause we're the best
Team of them all.
We always <u>beat</u>
The other players.
That's why we're called
The Dragon Slayers.

Activity 3 | Mnemonics for Verb Types

Lesson 1: State-of-Being Verbs

Objectives	To make a smooth transition between action and state-of-being verbs—which can be helping verbs; to get an understanding of state-of-being verbs into students' long-term memory
Time	One 40-minute class period
Materials	● overhead transparency with several model sentences containing state-of-being verbs (see below)

Step-by-Step

1. Show students the following sentences on an overhead transparency:

   I am a dragon lover.

   The real beast is the teacher.

   Thirty-two dragons were in the cafeteria.

   Eastern and Western dragons are very different.

2. Ask students to stand at their desks and act out the verbs in the sentences. Remind students to silently ask themselves, "What can I do in this sentence?" before they attempt to act out the verb. (When the activity begins, students may be confused. Then some students may try to act out the nouns, such as beast.)

3. After students attempt to act out the verbs, seat them and ask them why they could not physically demonstrate the verbs. Guide students to understand that the verbs in these sentences are state-of-being verbs; they simply state that something is or exists. Have students identify the verbs in the sentences.

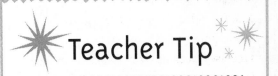

Teacher Tip

Remind students that to put information into long-term memory, they need to overlearn it. This validates the procedure for memorizing different verb types, and it helps students who memorize information quickly to understand why repetition and reinforcement are necessary.

4. Unlike action verbs, state-of-being verbs must be memorized. Teach students this mnemonic for state-of-being verbs:

   Ann is a wild, wonderful bouncing baby bear.

   Or, use it as a model to help students create an original mnemonic.

5. Show the sentence on the overhead. Read the whole sentence first. Then say, "'Ann' stands for *am*; 'Is' stands for *is*...." Have students echo you. Use this process with the remaining words in the sentence. Emphasize the /m/ in *am*; otherwise, students might confuse it with *an*. Repeat this two or three times, speeding up the pace as you go and allowing students to respond in unison as you point to each word.

6. Point to each word and have students say the state-of-being verb associated with it: "Ann, am." Each time you add a different pair of words, ask students to repeat all the pairs in front of it. For example, after students say, "Wild, was," point to the words "Ann, am" and have students say these words as well as "is, is" and "a, are."

7. Turn off the overhead projector and have students stand and say the sentence and the state-of-being verbs to a partner.

Ann	is	a	wild,	wonderful	bouncing	baby	bear.
m	s	r	a	e	e	e	e
		e	s	r		i	e
				e		n	e
						g	n

Variation

Have a mini contest. Allow students to see if they can say the sentence and the verbs without looking at the overhead. Award bonus points or a small prize to the volunteers. Narrow the time frame for the repetition. Ask, "Who can recite the state-of-being verbs in fifteen seconds? Ten?" Making a game out of the mnemonic really motivates students to learn.

Lesson 2: Helping Verbs

Objective	To introduce the concept of helping verbs with a song, sung to the tune of "Jingle Bells"
Time	One 40-minute class period
Materials	● copies of song sheets (one per student) and an overhead transparency of "The Helping Verbs Song" (below)

Step-by-Step

1. Ask students to hum a bar of "Jingle Bells," and then sing a rousing rendition of this well-known tune.

2. Sing "The Helping Verbs Song" until everyone is so familiar with the words that they can sing it to a partner.

3. For homework, ask students to practice the song so they can sing it from memory the next day. (Try a "sing off" contest, such as boys versus girls, or row one versus row two.)

The Helping Verbs Song

(sing to the tune of "Jingle Bells")

Do, does, did.

Have, has, had.

May . . . might . . . must.

Would, could, should.

Will, shall, can.

These are helping verbs!

Multiple Intelligences, Learning Styles, and Verbs

Objective	To evaluate students' understanding of verbs
Time	One 40-minute class period
Materials	● copies (one per student) of the activity sheet (page 44)
	● copies (one per student) of the rubric (page 45)
	● construction paper ● markers ● rulers ● scissors ● glue

The Purpose of These Activities

In the book *So Each May Learn*, the authors advocate integrating two learning models—the multiple intelligences, which addresses the *content* of learning, and learning styles, which focus on the *process* of learning. They delineate four basic learning styles: mastery, understanding, self-expressive, and interpersonal. Basically, mastery learners "seek to master skill and content" (Silver, Strong, & Perini, 2000, p. 25) whereas understanding learners enjoy exploring ideas, abstractions, and theories. Self-expressive learners rely on their intuition to guide them, prefer open-ended questions, and tend to be intrapersonal. Interpersonal learners are social and gregarious individuals who need to connect what they learn to personal experiences. The Multiple Intelligences, Learning Styles, and Verbs activities were developed in response to this integrated learning model. In the bibliography, you will find a list of resources to help you investigate students' multiple intelligences and learning styles.

> **Multiple Intelligences** Howard Gardner defines the eight intelligences as verbal-linguistic, math-logic, spatial, musical, bodily-kinesthetic, interpersonal, intrapersonal, and naturalist. Simply stated, human beings have the capacity to be word smart, logic smart, picture smart, music smart, body smart, people smart, self smart, and nature smart (Armstrong, 1994).

Step-by-Step

1. Acquaint students with both the multiple intelligences and learning styles.

2. Distribute the Multiple Intelligences, Learning Styles, and Verbs reproducible to students. Allow them to choose one of the options as their final assessment for the verb unit.

3. Use the Multiple Intelligences, Learning Styles, and Verbs rubric to evaluate students' work.

Sample Student Responses:

Spatial, Self-Expressive

My name is Ver Barian. I came up with a way to describe actions like bolting. The word for it is a verb, and I came up with this word with my first name plus my last initial.

Musical, Understanding

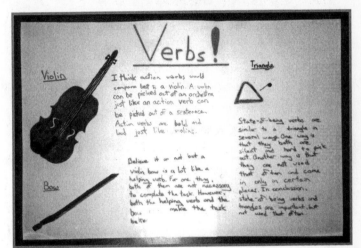

Teacher Tip

Students' Reactions to the Integrated Assessment

When I surveyed students to discover their attitudes toward the integrated assessment for verbs, which I referred to as the "the test," their reactions were overwhelmingly positive. One student wrote that the assessment "let me think and imagine things that I usually don't on a test." Another responded, "Most tests are not fun and give us stress, but this test was really fun and relaxing." Students' comments and reflections suggest that the options presented actually motivate and encourage them to express what they have learned.

Naturalist, Mastery

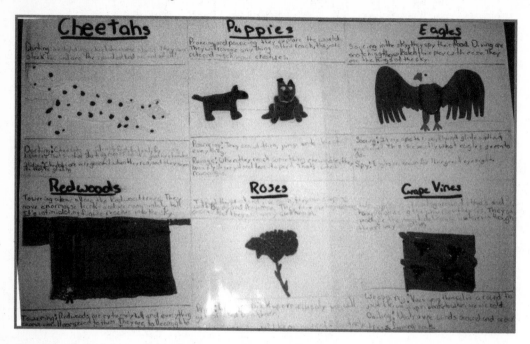

"Darting and gliding, cheetahs roam about. They have sleek fur and are the speediest animals of all!"

Why the Student Chose the Verbs

Darting: Cheetahs are extremely fast, but only for short distances. That's what darting means, so it is good for cheetahs.

Gliding: Cheetahs are very graceful when they run, and they seem like they're gliding.

Teacher's Note: Although the student uses "darting" and "gliding" as participles, she demonstrates a clear understanding of action verbs. Her explanations show she understands the use and meaning of darting and gliding as action verbs. Also, participles are verb forms which, as a sixth grader, the student has not studied.

Name: _____ Date: _____ Final Score: _____

Vivid Verb Cheer Rubric

Directions: Write the score for each area of assessment in the appropriate blank. Add the points together to determine the score.

Vivid Verbs
4–Contains five underlined powerful, vivid verbs.
3–Contains five underlined action verbs.
2–Verbs are not underlined and/or are overused.
1–Contains boo-hisser or state-of-being verbs.

_____ Peer _____ Teacher

Volume
4–Hear it in the stands!
3–Loud and clear.
2–Hear some words.
1–Close to a whisper.

_____ Peer _____ Teacher

Pronunciation
4–Enunciates!
3–Clearly recognize words.
2–Somewhat garbled.
1–Mumbles.

_____ Peer _____ Teacher

Tone of Voice
4–Supercharged!
3–Animated.
2–Normal.
1–Flat or monotone.

_____ Peer _____ Teacher

Pace
4–We can keep up!
3–Rarely goes too fast or slow.
2–Often goes too fast or slow.
1–Definitely too fast or slow.

_____ Peer _____ Teacher

Actions
4–Match verbs.
3–Usually match verbs.
2–Rarely fit verbs.
1–Little or no action.

_____ Peer _____ Teacher

Eye Contact
4–Always looks at audience.
3–Usually looks at audience.
2–Rarely looks at audience.
1–No eye contact.

_____ Peer _____ Teacher

Engages Audience
4–Definite interaction.
3–Audience shows interest.
2–Interest comes and goes.
1–Little or no interest.

_____ Peer _____ Teacher

Total Points Possible: 32

Peer Points: _____ + Teacher Points: _____ ÷ 2 = _____ Final Score

Peer Comments: _____

Teacher Comments: _____

Multiple Intelligences, Learning Styles, and Verbs

Directions: Complete one of the following activities to complete to show how well you understand verbs. You may need a separate piece of notebook paper to develop your response, or you may need to use construction paper, markers, rulers, scissors, or glue.

When making your choice, think about the intelligences and learning styles each option addresses. Choose the one that you think fits your learning profile. Circle your choice.

1. **Logical–Mathematical, Understanding:** Compare and contrast action, state-of-being, and helping verbs. Use a Venn diagram or another type of graphic organizer to show your comparisons. Include a written explanation of your comparisons.

2. **Spatial, Self–Expressive:** Create a cartoon that shows how the three different kinds of verbs came into being.

3. **Intrapersonal, Spatial, Verbal–Linguistic, Self–Expressive:** How does it feel to be a verb? Imagine that you are a verb. Use pictures and words to illustrate what your life is like. Include examples of action, state-of-being, and helping verbs.

4. **Verbal–Linguistic, Interpersonal:** With a partner, conduct an interview with Grandpa Verb. One of you will assume the role of the interviewer and will write questions for Grandpa to answer, the other responds as Grandpa. Be sure Grandpa explains the relationships among his children (the action verbs), his grandchildren (the helping verbs), and his great-grandchildren (the state-of-being verbs).

5. **Verbal–Linguistic, Logical–Mathematical, Mastery:** Make three columns on a sheet of paper. List five examples of each verb type in the appropriate column. Explain what these verbs do and why they are used.

6. **Musical, Understanding:** Choose a musical instrument to represent each verb type we have studied. Explain the relationship between the instrument and the verb type it represents.

7. **Naturalist, Mastery:** Use verbs to describe three animals and three plants. Include examples of action, state-of-being, and helping verbs in your descriptions. Choose two of the verbs in your descriptions and explain why they are the best verbs you could use to describe your plant or animal.

Name: _____ Date: _____ Final Score: _____

Rubric for Multiple Intelligences, Learning Styles, and Verbs

Directions: Circle the score for each area of assessment. Then use the rating system to determine the overall rating.

Content Depth

4–Substantial knowledge of verb types and their uses; many examples.

3–Adequate knowledge of verb types and their uses; some examples.

2–Limited knowledge of verb types and their uses; few examples.

1–Little knowledge of verb types and their uses; missing examples.

Appearance

4–Eye-catching; legible; goes above and beyond.

3–Noticeable attention to detail; neat; readable.

2–Moderate attention to detail; somewhat neat and readable.

1–Sloppy; not neat.

Mechanics (grammar, punctuation, capitalization, spelling)

4–Excellent mechanics; one or two errors.

3–Moderate number of mechanical errors.

2–Frequent errors; ideas can still be understood.

1–Filled with errors; ideas cannot be understood.

Creativity

4–Imaginative; unique point of view or approach.

3–Includes some interesting ideas and insights; somewhat original.

2–Few original ideas or insights.

1–Simply restates ideas and information; not original.

Rating Levels: 4 = Advanced   3 = Proficient   2= Basic   1 = Below Basic

---

To determine the overall rating level for the project:

4 = all 4's

3 = 3's or 3's and 4's with only one 1 or one 2

2 = two or more 2's

1 = two or more 1's

Savory Sentences

Once students understand the nuances of nouns and verbs, they are ready to connect this knowledge to the sentence. Activities such as the *Great Sentence Caper, Sentence Caricatures,* and *Recipe for a Sensational Sentence* capitalize on students' multiple intelligences, specifically targeting the verbal-linguistic, spatial, mathematical-logical, and bodily-kinesthetic intelligences. To involve students in learning, consider using what can be called the "discovery method" to begin a sentence unit. For example, if you teach about the four types of sentences during an interdisciplinary unit on oceanography, compose humorous sentences related to sea creatures or a field trip to the aquarium. To personalize the sentences, use the names of your school's students and teachers.

Involving Students How can we involve students in learning? Brooks and Brooks (1993), proponents of the constructivist theory, advocate that student-centered, inquiry-based methods of instruction engage learners.

Here are some sample themes and sentences you might use for the following sentence types:

Sentence Type	Theme	Sentence Examples
Declarative	Student Falls Into Fish Tank	At the aquarium a student fell into the fish tank.
		The soaked child looked surprised.
Interrogative	Principal Swallowed by a Whale	Are you sure the whale swallowed the principal?
		Do you think our heroic leader is scared in there?
Imperative	Sea Commands	Watch out for the prickly puffer fish!
		Eat yummy eel stew.
Exclamatory	Giant Squid Attacks Teacher	A giant squid is attacking the teacher!
		She is stuck to its enormous suction cups!

Activity 1 Classifying Sentences

Objectives	To classify the four kinds of sentences; to analyze and list the characteristics of the four kinds of sentences
Time	One or two 40-minute class periods
Materials	● one 12" x 18" card or sentence strip per student; each one with an example of one of the four different sentence types (declarative, interrogative, exclamatory, and imperative) ● chart paper (one piece per group) ● markers for each student ● sets of four different colored index cards (one set per student)

Step-by-Step

1. After creating the sentence strips, place one facedown on students' desks.

2. After all students receive a card, ask them to turn it over and read it. Explain to students that they will form four groups based on similarities in the themes and sentences on their cards. Provide a brief overview of the themes.

3. Direct students to stand up, hold up their cards, move around the room, and find the other cards to which they relate. Coach and question students to assist them in this process.

4. Have the groups move to four different sections of the room (I use my four corners), sit in a circle, and take turns reading and showing their cards to each other.

5. Tell students to search for and discuss similarities in the sentences. Write these questions on the board to assist them in the discovery process:

   How do the sentences begin?

   How do the sentences end?

   What kind of job does each sentence do?

   What other kinds of similarities do you notice?

6. Give each group a piece of chart paper and each student a marker. Have the members take turns writing the similarities.

7. Call one group at a time to the front of the room. Have each group member read his or her sentence out loud. Have the rest of the class identify the similarities among the sentences. Pose questions to elicit relevant information.

8. After each group presentation and discussion, have one group member read the chart summarizing the characteristics of the sentence type. Add new information from the discussion to the list. Ask students if they can name the sentence type described. If they cannot, assist them. Collect the cards or strips after each group presents.

9. Distribute one set of colored index cards and one marker to each student. Designate a color to represent a sentence type, for example, pink for imperative, blue for exclamatory, green for interrogative, and yellow for declarative.

10. With colored markers, have students draw the end punctuation mark for each sentence type on the front side of the index card and the sentence type, example, and definition on the back. Use the charts the groups created and sentence strips or cards to guide this process.

11. For retention, show examples of the four sentence types on the overhead projector; however, do not add end punctuation to the sentences. Direct students to identify the sentence type by holding up the appropriate index card after you say, "One, two, three, show me." This command prevents students from piggybacking on each other's answers.

Exclamatory

The teacher just flipped a giant squid!

Definition: Exclamatory sentences show strong emotion and end with an exclamation point.

Variation

Use movement to reinforce the concept of the four kinds of sentences as you show examples of them on the overhead. Students should stand beside their desks as they do each motion described below.

Declarative: Students form a period (a big "o") with their thumb and index finger and say, "Declarative—makes a statement."

Interrogative: Students look puzzled, scratch their heads, and say, "Huh? Interrogative—asks a question."

Imperative: As students salute, they say, "Imperative—gives an order."

Exclamatory: Using both hands, students literally make their hair stand on end and then say, "Exclamatory—shows emotion."

Awesome Hands-on Activities for Teaching Grammar

Activity 2 The Great Sentence Caper

Objectives	To review the four kinds of sentences; to use the four kinds of sentences in an original script; to use speaking and performance skills to present plays
Time	Two 40-minute class periods
Materials	◉ an overhead transparency of The Case of the Missing Dentures (page 61) ◉ paper ◉ pencils ◉ props (optional)

Step-by-Step

1. Provide an overview of the assignment. Explain to students that they will work in small groups to compose an original mini mystery play that uses the four kinds of sentences. Write the following guidelines on the board and review them with students:

   • Crimes must be humorous, not violent.

   • The cast of characters might include a detective, a witness, and a victim.

   • Each character in the play should represent one of the four sentence types. For example, Matter-of-Fact Mike, an eyewitness in the crime, uses only declarative sentences.

2. Brainstorm and dialogue with students about some potential topics for the crimes and list them on the board. Here are some suggestions:

   • The Case of the Chocolate Burglar

   • The Case of the Missing Teacher

   • The Case of the Lost Lip Gloss

   • The Case of the Hope Diamond Heist

3. To model the assignment, show a transparency of The Case of the Missing Dentures on the overhead projector. Emphasize that a sixth grader wrote this. Before you read the script out loud, explain voice intonation and inflection. Model this as you read. Afterward, ask students which character represents each sentence type. Have them support their answers with examples from the text.

4. Form groups of four students, making adjustments where necessary. For example, in a group of three, have one person be two characters.

5. List the group goals for the day on the board:

- Choose a crime.

- Write the script. Take turns sharing ideas for the sentences. Everyone records so that all group members have a script to memorize.

- Use at least eight lines of dialogue, two lines per character.

- Make a list of props.

6. Allow time for students to write the scripts.

7. During the second class period, have students finish writing the scripts, practice their lines, and perform the plays. (I allow students to use their scripts during the plays because I want them to concentrate on voice inflection and intonation, not memorization.)

8. After each performance, ask the audience which kind of sentence each student represents in the skit. Students must give a reason for their response.

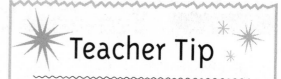

Teacher Tip

After teaching the four kinds of sentences, ask students to analyze a piece of their own writing to determine whether it has a variety of sentences. Have them highlight declarative sentences in yellow, exclamatory in blue, interrogative in green, and imperative in pink. Ask them to count how many of each sentence type they have. The color-coding allows most students to immediately see that they need to vary their sentence structure. Next, have students revise and change three or four declarative sentences into other sentence types. Model how to do this first. Older students can use this process with simple, compound, and complex sentences.

Awesome Hands-on Activities for Teaching Grammar

Activity 3 | Sentence Caricatures

Objective	To create a caricature designed to represent one of the four sentence types
Time	One 40-minute class period
Materials	● 9" x 12" white construction paper (one piece per student)
	● colored pencils ● crayons ● markers ● rulers

Step-by-Step

1. Have students draw an original cartoon-like character that relates to one of the four sentence types or to the different punctuation marks that accompany the four kinds of sentences. For example, a figure representing exclamatory sentences might have hair that stands on end. His eyes and mouth could be wide open and O-shaped. On his chest he might have a huge heart because he is full of emotion.

2. Distribute the construction paper. Ask students to hold it lengthwise and write the name of their caricature at the top of the page in large, printed letters. The name should relate to the sentence type represented, such as Declarative Dan or Hysterical Helen.

3. Beneath and around the caricature, have students write five examples of the sentence type represented.

4. You may want to award prizes, such as Most Humorous, Best Representation, and Most Creative. To grade the caricatures, consider using this simple evaluation sheet:

Four Kinds of Sentences Evaluation Sheet

Criteria	Points Possible	Points Earned
Caricature clearly represents the sentence type.	10	_____
Poster includes five examples of the sentence type.	10	_____
Poster has name of sentence type/character.	5	_____
All spelling is correct.	5	_____
Project is neat, colored, and proportionate.	5	_____

Activity 4 # Introducing Subjects and Predicates

Objective	To introduce subjects and predicates in sentences containing a subject that definitively relates to a single predicate
Time	10 to 15 minutes
Materials	● strips of laminated paper in two different colors, containing subjects and predicates that can be combined to make sentences (one sentence per student pair)

Step-by-Step

1. Give students a subject or predicate strip. Have them find their "match" or "other half."

2. As soon as they find their partner, have them answer the following questions:

   When you are together, what do you make? Why are you in two parts?

   Why do you need each other? How do you begin? How do you end?

3. Once students discover that they have made sentences, and that together they have a subject and a verb, call pairs of students to the front of the room. Ask the class to use two questions to find the pair's verb:

   Can I do anything in this sentence? Are there any special verbs I've memorized?

   Remind them to always find the verb first. Since the sentence strips are laminated, whoever finds the verb can underline it twice with an overhead transparency marker.

4. Have students find the subject by asking "who" or "what" about the verb. Have whoever finds the subject underline it once. Then have students find the complete predicate (the verb plus everything that goes along with it) and the complete subject (the noun and/or pronoun plus everything that goes along with it/them).

5. After each presentation, have students clean the sentence strips and collect them.

6. Proceed through the remaining sentences at a rapid pace to help students internalize the strategy for finding simple and complete subjects and predicates.

Teacher Tips

For this introductory activity, I use action verbs exclusively. For example, "Forty-two police officers jailed the English teacher for poor grammar."

Use strips of one color for subjects and another color for predicates:

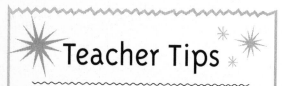

Plump pink pigs
(blue subject strip)

oink in the pen.
(pink predicate strip)

Silly Subjects and Perky Predicates

Objective	To identify simple and complete subjects and predicates
Time	10 to 15 minutes
Materials	● copies (one per student pair) of Silly Subjects and Perky Predicates cards (page 62) ● envelopes labeled Silly Subjects and Perky Predicates (one per student pair) ● overhead projector markers (one per student pair) ● spray bottles filled with water ● paper towels ● an overhead transparency of the answer key (use a copy of the reproducible with the verbs underlined twice and the simple subjects underlined once)

Step-by-Step

1. Enlarge, copy, cut out, and laminate the Silly Subjects and Perky Predicates cards and place one set of cards into its labeled envelope.

2. Assign each student a partner. Then distribute one envelope containing the subjects and predicates, one overhead transparency marker, and one or two paper towels to each pair of students. Place a spray bottle near groups of students and ask them to share it.

3. Have partners take turns matching the subjects to the predicates. Partners should use the questioning strategy (Can I do anything in this sentence? Are there any special verbs I've memorized?) to find the verbs or simple predicate. With an overhead transparency marker, students can underline the verbs twice.

4. Have students use the questioning strategy (ask who or what about the verb) to find the simple subject. With an overhead projector marker, students can underline the simple subject once.

5. Have students identify and read the complete predicates and the complete subjects.

6. When students complete the activity, show the answer key on the overhead projector.

7. Have students clean the cards, and then mix them and return them to the envelopes. Then collect the envelopes.

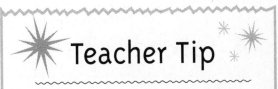

Teacher Tip

To internalize the process for finding subjects and predicates, students must think out loud and use the questioning strategy. As students engage in the Silly Subjects and Perky Predicates activity, circulate around the room to make sure they are applying the strategy. Internalizing the strategy significantly helps students when the task becomes more difficult and they are confronted with compound and complex sentences or sentences with subjects in unusual positions.

Activity 6 — Recipe for a Sensational Sentence

Part 1: Teacher Demonstration

Objectives	To reinforce the concepts of subject, predicate, and sentence structure by having students use food to demonstrate what they know about the parts of a sentence and sentence types; to construct a model of a sentence; to use five of the eight multiple intelligences: mathematical-logical, verbal-linguistic, spatial, interpersonal, and bodily-kinesthetic
Time	5 to 10 minutes
Materials	● chefs' hats ● apron ● mixing bowl ● large spoon ● omelette pan ● six plastic eggs (label one of these "complete thought") Cover the following items in aluminum foil, construction paper, or contact paper and label them accordingly: ● large salt or oatmeal container labeled "Salty Subject" ● large pepper container or cereal box labeled "Peppery Predicate" ● two spice containers or one milk and one cream carton labeled "Nouns" and "Pronouns" (fill these containers with five nouns and five pronouns written on construction paper) ● One spice container labeled "Vivid Verbs" (fill this with five verbs written on construction paper)

Step-by-Step

1. In the front of the classroom, on a flat table or cart, set up a "cooking station." Wear a chef's hat and apron. Put all of the materials for the demonstration in the cooking station.

2. Tell the class that today you are preparing the dish known as the "Sensational Sentence Omelette." Put as much gusto, humor, and enthusiasm into your performance as possible. The dialogue might sound something like this:

   "Today we will prepare an exquisite Sensational Sentence Omelette. How shall I begin?"

   (Crack one or two eggs into the mixing bowl.)

   "I know! First I need a Salty Subject."

   (Hold up the Salty Subject container; pretend to pour some into the bowl; stir vigorously.)

   "But what ingredients go into the Salty Subject?"

   (Look puzzled.)

   "Who can tell me?"

3. Select one or two volunteers to come up to the front and add nouns and pronouns to the bowl. Ask them to read the words out loud as they put them into the bowl. When they come forward, crown them with a chef's hat. As they drop the words into the bowl, stir vigorously so that the words fly out of the bowl. Grab them, reread them out loud, and put them back into the bowl.

4. Continue the dramatization, adding the Peppery Predicate and Vivid Verbs to the mixing bowl. As you put the mixture into the omelette pan, say:

   "I think I am forgetting something. I wonder what it could be?"

5. When a student volunteer offers the words, "A complete thought," pull out the complete thought egg and add it to the omelette.

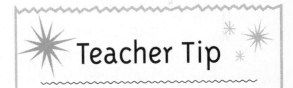

Teacher Tip

Purchase paper chefs' hats at a local party and food store for about one dollar each.

Part 2: Student Activity

Objectives	To demonstrate knowledge of the sentence parts and types; to follow directions for making a recipe; to use higher-order thinking skills, specifically analogy and comparison, to compare the parts of a sentence to ingredients in a recipe
Time	30 minutes
Materials	● quart-size plastic bags (one per pair of students) filled with the following:

1 saltine cracker	1 piece of shoestring licorice
1 pretzel	1 M&M®
4 or 5 mini marshmallows	1 toothpick
4 or 5 raisins	1 gumdrop
1 alphabet cereal capital letter	1 plastic knife to spread the icing

● two cans of ready-made icing ● paper plates (one per student pair) with a tablespoon of icing on the edge of each ● copies (one per student) of Recipe for a Sensational Sentence (page 63) ● adhesive tape ● index cards ● toothpicks ● scissors (one per student pair)

Step-by-Step

1. Pair students. Tell students that today they are going to be chefs. Their job is to prepare the Recipe for a Sensational Sentence.

2. Distribute one plastic bag, one paper plate with icing (students use the plates as the base for constructing the models), two copies of Recipe for a Sensational Sentence, one index card, and one pair of scissors to each pair. Put the rolls of tape near students.

3. Explain that students are to follow all of the directions on the Recipe for a Sensational Sentence activity page.

4. After students make their sentences, ask them to use the index card, scissors, and tape to label all the parts of the sentence. Encourage students to give specific examples of simple and complete subjects and predicates, nouns, pronouns, verbs, and sentence types. Their goal is to demonstrate

as much knowledge about the sentence as they can through their labels.

5. Circulate around the room. Encourage students to add more detail to their labels by asking questions.

6. When students complete the activity, have the partners explain their models. Be sure to allow students to enjoy consuming the sentence.

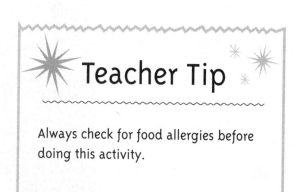

Teacher Tip

Always check for food allergies before doing this activity.

Follow Up

For homework, ask students to create an original recipe for a sentence on large 12" x 18" construction paper, which you provide. Emphasize that they are not allowed to use the ingredients from Recipe for a Sensational Sentence.

Ask students to include the following on their posters:

- a list of all ingredients needed to make a sentence
- pictures of the ingredients
- labels for each picture showing what each ingredient represents
- directions for combining the ingredients to make a sentence

Allow two nights for students to complete this project. Because the project truly demonstrates understanding of the parts of a sentence and the sentence types, have students keep these posters in their portfolios.

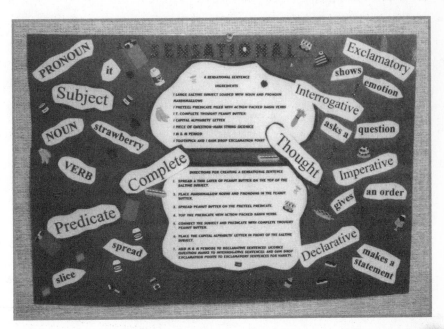

Activity 7 Words in Unusual Positions

Objectives	To identify subjects and predicates in unusual positions using a think-aloud strategy; to reinforce the think-aloud strategy using manipulatives
Time	10 to 15 minutes
Materials	(For Strategy 3: Magnificent Manipulatives)
	● sets of sentences described in Strategy 3, Step 1 (one per group of four students, copied on card stock and laminated) ● hook-and-loop fasteners
	● sets (one per group of four students) of Subjects in Unusual Positions word cards (page 64) ● resealable plastic sandwich bags to hold the word cards
	● paper clips ● an overhead transparency of the answer key for the activity

Strategy 1: The Think-Aloud: Identifying Subjects After Verbs

Step-by-Step

1. Share the script at right with students and model the strategy.

2. Then have students work with a partner and use the strategy to find verbs and subjects in a series of practice sentences. Make sure they actually say each step out loud and then do it. (Thinking out loud helps students internalize the process for finding subjects in unusual positions.)

The Sentence: There are the children.

Step 1: Find the verb.

    Ask: What can I do in this sentence?

    Answer: I cannot do anything.

    Ask: Are there any special verbs I have memorized?

    Answer: Yes, I memorized *are*.

    The verb = are

Step 2: Find the simple subject.

    Ask: Who or what are?

    Answer: Children are.

    The simple subject = children

Strategy 2: The Think-Aloud: Identifying Subjects in Interrogative Sentences

1. Share the following script with students and model the strategy.

2. Then have students work with a partner and use the strategy to find verbs and subjects in a series of practice sentences. Make sure they actually say each step out loud and then do it. (Thinking out loud helps students internalize the process for finding subjects in unusual positions.)

The Sentence: Did you see the movie?

Step 1: Rewrite the question to make it a statement.

Rewrite: You did see the movie.

Step 2: Find the verb.

Ask: What can I do in this sentence?

Answer: I can see.

Ask: Are there any special verbs I have memorized?

Answer: Yes, I memorized the verb *did*.

The verb = did see

Step 3: Find the simple subject.

Ask: Who or what did see?

Answer: You did see.

The simple subject = you

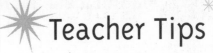

Teacher Tips

It can be a struggle to successfully teach students how to find subjects in sentences with unusual word order. Physically manipulating the words and using a think-aloud strategy truly help students understand this difficult, abstract concept.

To teach the think-aloud strategy, use direct instruction. Vary the instructional approach by using the overhead projector and transparencies, a Smartboard®, a PowerPoint® presentation, or student response boards.

Strategy 3: Magnificent Manipulatives

Step-by-Step

1. Type each sentence below in a large font on a separate page, orienting the page horizontally. Beneath each sentence, create one square box for every word in the sentence (see example below):

   Sentence 1: Have you seen Gregory Gorilla?

   Sentence 2: There are his footprints.

   Sentence 3: Did the huge gorilla escape?

   Sentence 4: Through the city zoo he thundered.

   Sentence 5: Where could the gorilla be?

   Sentence 6: Is he in room 320?

2. On card stock, copy enough sets of the six sentences so that each group of four students has a set. Laminate the cards.

3. Place a piece of hook-and-loop fastener (use the soft side) in the center of each box on every card.

4. On card stock, enlarge, copy, cut, and laminate the Subjects in Unusual Positions word cards.

5. Place a piece of hook-and-loop fastener on the back of each word card (use the rough side).

6. Put the word cards for each sentence in a separate sandwich bag. Paper clip the bags to the corresponding sentence card to assemble complete sets.

7. Form groups of four students and distribute one set of sentence and word cards to each group.

8. Write the following student directions for the activity on the board:

   Distribute one sentence and one set of word cards to each group member.

   Taking turns, each person in the group:

   - reads the sentence on the card out loud.

   - rearranges the word cards from the plastic bag to create a sentence in which the subject comes in front of the verb.

   - attaches the word cards to the sentence card.

   - asks the appropriate questions to find the verb(s).

   - asks "who" or "what" about the verb to find the subject.

   - states the complete subject and the complete predicate.

9. Before they work independently, have students collectively practice the steps listed above with sentences 1 and 2. Model the process first.

10. Review the answers on the overhead.

11. Clean up and collect the cards.

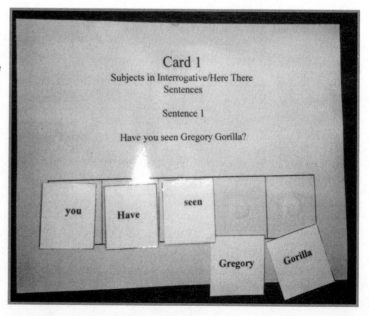

Awesome Hands-on Activities for Teaching Grammar

The Case of the Missing Dentures

By Deneille R.

Scene One: Grandma and Grandpa Weezer's House

Grandpa Weezer: Honey darlin', I can't find my dentures! They're not in the Alka Seltzer jar!

Grandma Weezer: Look in the sink, toilet, and your cereal bowl.

Grandpa Weezer: I'm going to call the cops! I've got bingo tonight!

(Grandpa calls the police. Cop Megalopolis arrives.)

Cop Megalopolis: Grandpa, why did you wake me up?

Grandpa Weezer: I lost my dentures! I lost my dentures!

Grandma Weezer: Go check the bingo hall.

(Grandma, Grandpa, Megalopolis, and Cupcake, the dog, go to the bingo hall.)

Scene Two: The Bingo Hall

Cop Megalopolis: Seymour, where were you last night? What were you doing? What time was it?

Seymour: We were just playing bingo with our old bud Weezer around 7:30 last night.

Grandpa Weezer: All I was doing was playing with my dog Cupcake!

Seymour: I remember taking Weezer home and noticing his dog's bright, white teeth.

Cop Megalopolis: Why doesn't someone go check Cupcake's mouth?

Grandma Weezer: Open your mouth now, Cupcake.

Grandpa Weezer: There are my perfect pearly teeth! Now I can finally eat!

Silly Subjects and Perky Predicates

The prickly porcupine	poked a pirate.
Big, brawny baboons	beat their chests.
The angry anteater	ate too many fire ants.
The loud, laughing hyena	giggled uncontrollably.
The gigantic giraffe	munched tree leaves.
The scared skunk	sprayed Sally.
The odd octopus	grew seven legs, not eight.
Plump pink pigs	oink in the pen.
Cranky cats	hiss and mew loudly.
Porky penguins	waddle on walks.

Recipe for a Sensational Sentence

Steps for Creating a Sensational Sentence

Step 1:   Collect all of the ingredients for the recipe.

Step 2:   Follow the directions for creating a sensational sentence.

Step 3:   Use toothpicks, adhesive tape, and index cards to label all the parts of the Sensational Sentence. Include examples of subjects, predicates, parts of speech, and sentence types.

Step 4:   Show the teacher your finished product. Explain it to him or her.

Step 5:   Enjoy eating the sentence!

Ingredients

1 large saltine cracker subject loaded with noun and pronoun marshmallows
1 pretzel predicate piled with action-packed raisin verbs
1 tbsp. Complete Thought icing
1 capital alphabet cereal letter
1 piece of question-mark string licorice
1 M&M® period
1 toothpick and 1 gumdrop exclamation point

Directions

1. Spread a thin layer of icing on the top of the saltine subject.

2. Place marshmallow nouns and pronouns in the icing.

3. Spread icing on the pretzel predicate.

4. Top the predicate with action-packed raisin verbs.

5. Place the saltine subject next to the pretzel predicate.

6. Connect the subject and predicate with Complete Thought icing.

7. Place the capital alphabet cereal letter in front of the saltine subject.

8. Add an M&M® period to a declarative sentence, a licorice question mark to an interrogative sentence, and a gumdrop exclamation point to an exclamatory sentence for variety. For an imperative sentence, punctuate with an M&M® period or a gumdrop exclamation point.

gorilla	escape	Through	in	room	320
Did	the	huge	be	Is	he
are	his	footprints	could	the	gorilla
Gregory	Gorilla	There	he	thundered	Where
Have	you	seen	the	city	zoo

Forget Fragments and Rule Out Run-ons

How do we teach students to recognize two grammatical bloopers—fragments and run-ons—in the context of their own writing? First, we need to motivate students to learn about the topic. Since novel tasks stimulate intrinsic motivation (Brandt, 1998), one approach is to use movement, social interaction, and unusual materials to spark student interest in fragments and run-ons. As brain research indicates, forging connections makes learning personally meaningful for students and also enhances understanding. Although the lessons and activities described below work well for students, the concept of correcting run-ons and fragments in student writing must be constantly reinforced to foster retention. Each time students revise, edit, and proofread, they revisit and repair fragments and run-ons. By the end of the school year, most students can identify and self-correct these problems in their own writing.

> **Movement** "Every lesson should include a kinesthetic activity. Only small percentages of any group of learners respond best to purely auditory stimuli" (Moss & Fuller, 2000, p. 274).

Activity 1 — Mini-Lesson for Fragments

Objective	To identify and correct fragments
Time	One 40-minute class period
Materials	● overhead projector ● overhead transparencies of fragments (pages 65 and 66)
	● overhead transparency markers ● dry-erase board for each student
	● dry-erase markers ● spray bottles filled with water ● paper towels

Step-by-Step

1. To create sentences for the fragment demonstration, choose an amusing topic. (I write about the two hamsters that actually escaped from the cage in our science room.)

2. Show several fragments on the overhead. You can include humorous drawings, graphics, and sound effects—and even puppets to dramatize some of the sentences. This novel approach truly motivates and engages students.

3. Ask students whether these words are sentences, discuss why they are not, and define the term *fragment*.

Examples of Fragments:

Esmerelda and Zelda, two happy hamsters.

Enjoy playing pranks.

The innocent science teacher.

4. Show a single fragment on the overhead. Model how to correct a fragment by adding words.

Example of Adding Words to Fix a Fragment:

Fragment: Buried themselves under wood chips.

Sentence: The two hamsters buried themselves under wood chips.

5. Distribute dry-erase boards and markers to students. Revealing one at a time, show three more examples of fragments.

Examples of Fragments for Students to Correct by Adding Words:

One tiny prankster in the science room.

Searching high and low for the little imps.

No new toys for the hamsters today.

6. Ask students to fix each one by adding words. While a student volunteer corrects the fragments on the overhead transparency, have the remaining students make their corrections on dry-erase boards. Review the volunteers' answers as a whole class. Seated students exchange dry-erase boards with each other to check for complete sentences. If there are any questions about corrections, serve as the final evaluator.

7. Next, model how to correct fragments by combining thoughts.

Examples of Correcting Fragments by Combining Thoughts:

Fragment: After trembling in her socks.

Sentence: The science teacher shrieked.

Correction: After trembling in her socks, the science teacher shrieked.

8. Following the same procedure outlined in Step 4, have students repair the following fragments by combining thoughts:

Fragment: When they spied the teacher crawling.

Sentence: The two imps began to giggle.

Fragment: After the teacher heard the noise.

Sentence: She sprinted toward it.

Sentence: The two hamsters snorted.

Fragment: As they laughed mischievously.

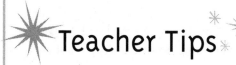

Teacher Tips

To make an inexpensive set of dry-erase boards, go to a home supply store for a large sheet of wipe-off shower board. Ask the store to cut it into squares. My set of thirty-two cost $12.00!

Incorporating technology can improve an introduction to fragments and run-ons. PowerPoint® presentations can be made more interactive with a wireless keyboard. Students then pass the keyboard around the room and use it to correct the fragments and run-ons in the PowerPoint® presentation. While one student corrects the errors on the slide, the others write their corrections on paper or dry-erase boards so that everyone in the class is involved in the activity.

Activity 2   Foil the Fragments

Objective	To identify and correct fragments
Time	20 to 25 minutes
Materials	● poster-size copies (one per group of 4) of Foil the Fragments (page 76) ● spray bottles (one per group) filled with water ● overhead transparency markers (one per group) ● paper towels ● an overhead transparency answer key for Foil the Fragments

Step-by-Step

1. Form groups of four and explain the following directions for the Foil the Fragments activity. (Write them on the board prior to class.)

   • When you receive your Foil the Fragments poster, read the whole story silently.

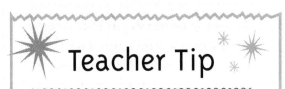

Teacher Tip

Turn this activity into a game. You might award groups one point for identifying each fragment and one point for correcting it, either with proofreading marks or by forming new sentences. Ask groups to write the total number of points earned at the top of the poster. The group with the highest number of points might earn a prize. I write each winner's name on a puzzle piece titled "Fragment Fixer." This puzzle piece serves as a "homework freebie." Instead of completing a five-point homework assignment, students give me the puzzle piece. My students love having one homework-free night!

• Next, take turns reading each sentence of the story out loud. After hearing each sentence, your group should vote by a show of hands to determine whether the group of words is a sentence or a fragment. Use the overhead transparency marker and the proper proofreading symbol (frag) and brackets to identify the fragments.

• After identifying all of the fragments, take turns correcting them with the overhead transparency marker. There are two ways to correct the errors:

   1. Add words to the fragment to make it a complete thought.

   2. Use proofreading symbols to connect sentences.

• When you are not fixing a fragment, observe, check, and encourage your teammates to be sure their corrections are accurate.

2. After the groups finish the activity, have each team exchange its poster with another team. Show the answer key on the overhead. Then ask the groups to check each correction.

Variation

Use the bodily-kinesthetic intelligence to demonstrate the difference between a sentence and a fragment. Ask students to stand beside their desks. Show examples of sentences and fragments on the overhead. Reveal the examples one at a time. Tell students that when they see a complete sentence, they are to make a circle with their hands, since a complete sentence is a whole or complete thought. If they see a fragment, they are to stand on their left foot while simultaneously raising their right arm above their head. This "hanging" gesture shows that a fragment just hangs there; it does not represent a complete thought. Students should do these motions only when you say, "one, two, three, show me."

Activity 3   Forget Fragments

Objective	To identify and correct fragments in students' writing
Time	One 40-minute class period
Materials	● large index cards (one for each student) ● 12" x 18" colored construction paper (one for each student) ● Student writing folders and/or a basket containing fragments from students' writing ● glue sticks ● scissors ● markers ● crayons ● colored pencils ● copies (one for each student) of the Rubric for the Forget Fragments Puzzle (page 77)

Step-by-Step

1. Have students review the work in their writing folders and select a fragment to correct, or have students select a fragment from a basket (provide samples for any students who do not keep writing samples in class or whose writing is typically fragment-free).

2. Distribute a large index card to each student. Have students draw two large puzzle pieces on the card and then cut them out.

3. On the left-hand puzzle piece, have students write their fragments.

4. On the right-hand piece, have students correct the fragments and write complete sentences.

5. Remind students to write the fragments in one color and the corrections in another color. Also, have them use a ruler to draw lightly penciled lines on the puzzle piece so that their writing will be neat (or have them write on the lined-side of the index card).

6. Have students decorate the puzzle pieces, glue them to the construction paper, and add a title to the project.

7. Display the puzzle pieces around the room and in the hallway. Use the Forget Fragments rubric to evaluate the projects.

Mini-Lesson for Run-ons

Objectives	To identify run-on sentences; to correct run-on sentences with semicolons; to correct run-on sentences with proper end punctuation and capitalization
Time	20 to 25 minutes
Materials	● overhead projector ● overhead transparencies of run-ons (pages 70 and 71) ● overhead transparency markers ● run-on sentences (one per student) from the overhead transparencies ● a puppet

Step-by-Step

1. Using any puppet you have available, fire one sentence after another at students. (I use Big Mouth Bob, my enormous fish puppet.) Have the puppet yammer through a run-on sentence such as this:

   Hi I'm Big Mouth Bob, the biggest blabber-mouth in town, so people tell me but I don't believe them I think they are jealous of me because I'm a happening dude who can spin a tale and entertain folks why just yesterday when I was downtown shopping some diamond-studded grandma's pet poodle grabbed hold of my tail with its razor-sharp itsy, bitsy teeth well I swatted my tail back and forth like a jet propeller but that feisty furball wouldn't budge.

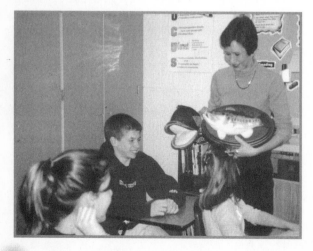

2. After such a dramatic introduction, gasp for breath and ask students to identify the grammar and writing problem you demonstrated. Once students identify the problem, follow the same procedure and process used to introduce fragments.

3. Revealing one at a time, show three examples of run-on sentences on the overhead. Model two ways to correct the first run-on: (1) by adding a semicolon, or (2) by using proper capitalization and end punctuation to create two or more sentences. Distribute a handout of the run-on sentences to students.

   Example of a Run-on:

   Run-on: I'm a happening dude who spins tales why just yesterday a pompous poodle grabbed my tail.

   Correction 1: I'm a happening dude who spins tales; why, just yesterday a pompous poodle grabbed my tail.

   Correction 2: I'm a happening dude who spins tales. Why, just yesterday a pompous poodle grabbed my tail.

4. Continue the mini-lesson by showing two more examples of run-ons. While a student volunteer corrects the run-ons on the overhead transparency, have the remaining students make their corrections on dry-erase boards. Review the corrections as a whole class.

Examples of Run-ons:

Run-on #1: That varmint's itsy, bitsy teeth sliced into me I shrieked and swatted my tail back and forth like a jet propeller.

Correction 1: That varmint's itsy, bitsy teeth sliced into me; I shrieked and swatted my tail back and forth like a jet propeller.

Correction 2: That varmint's itsy, bitsy teeth sliced into me. I shrieked and swatted my tail back and forth like a jet propeller.

Run-on #2: That feisty furball wouldn't budge then I spun in circles to launch it to Mars.

Correction 1: That feisty furball wouldn't budge; then I spun in circles to launch it to Mars.

Correction 2: That feisty furball wouldn't budge. Then I spun in circles to launch it to Mars.

Activity 5 Roll Out the Run-ons

Objective	To identify and correct run-on sentences
Time	30 minutes
Materials	● one laminated run-on sentence roll per group of four (prepare ahead of time using the example below and banner-length strips of paper)
	● blue overhead projector pens ● red overhead projector pens
	● spray bottles filled with water ● paper towels
	● overhead transparency answer key

Example Run-on Sentence

Oh no, here comes Big Mouth Bob he blabbers on and on like an overactive motor as soon as a warm body stands next to this chatterbox, he starts yammering why he never stops to take a breath in fact, last week when I bumped into Big Mouth, he began this long tale about how his shoelace got stuck in the escalator at the mall well, by the time he finished blubbering about his near escape from death, the sun had set if you ever see a freckle-faced dude with a whale-sized mouth, run for your life otherwise, you may be old and gray before Bob finishes talking to you.

Step-by-Step

1. Divide the class into teams of four. Assign each team a specific location that is large enough for them to roll out the run-ons. (Push desks against the walls so that you have enough room.)

2. Have team members sit in a square on the floor. Explain that teams will use proofreading symbols and punctuation to correct a gigantic run-on sentence.

3. Give each group a roll containing the enormous run-on, one blue overhead marker, one red overhead marker, one spray bottle filled with water, and two paper towels.

4. Tell the group to unroll the run-on, making sure it is facedown. Position a student at each end of the run-on. Have them flip the run-on face up after saying, "one, two, three, flip."

5. State that the four members of the team must silently read the entire run-on before they are allowed to make the corrections. As soon as all groups have finished reading, direct each group member to take a turn using the blue transparency marker, as well as

6. To keep track of the order in which groups complete the activity, give each group a numbered slip of paper as they finish.

proper proofreading symbols and punctuation, to correct the run-on. As one person corrects, the others make sure the answer is right.

7. Next, have students move to another group's run-on sentence. As you show the answers on the overhead transparency, students use the red transparency marker to correct the answers. You may want to award a small prize to the team that finished first and had 100 percent accuracy.

8. Have teams clean the strips. Remind students to squirt the paper towels with water, not the banner or the sentence strips.

Activity 6 | Commas for Compound Sentences

Objective	To identify and correct run-ons in compound sentences
Time	10 to 15 minutes
Materials	● one set per group of four of Commas for Compound Sentences (page 78)
	● envelopes labeled Commas for Compound Sentencess (one per group)
	● Grammar Rock video ● spray bottles filled with water (one per group)
	● overhead projector markers ● paper towels ● an overhead transparency of the answer key for Commas for Compound Sentences

Step-by-Step

1. Enlarge, copy, cut out, and laminate the sentence strips. Put them in their envelopes.

2. Before students can correct run-ons in compound sentences, they need to memorize the coordinating conjunctions. To review the conjunctions, have your class sing the song "Conjunction Junction" from the Schoolhouse Rock video titled *Grammar Rock*.

3. Once students know the conjunctions, show the following sentence on the overhead:

    Run-on: The math monster devours math books and he consumes calculators too.

4. Explain that this sentence is a run-on because it does not have a comma in front of the conjunction *and*, which connects two separate sentences.

    Correction: The math monster devours math books, and he consumes calculators too.

5. Show four more examples on the overhead and ask student volunteers to do the index finger test (see tip at right) for the class.

The math monster escaped from its cage and sneaked around the room.

The math teacher bellowed at the beast and she shrieked when the creature spouted incorrect answers.

The frustrated teacher chased the monster but could not catch it.

The shocked students shivered in their chairs or they screamed while standing on desktops.

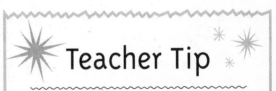

Teacher Tip

To test a sentence to see if it needs a comma in front of the conjunction, tell students to put their index finger over the conjunction. If they see a sentence in front of their finger and a second one behind their finger, they need to put a comma in front of the conjunction to avoid a run-on.

6. Next, form groups of four. Distribute one set of Commas for Compound Sentences, one spray bottle, and one overhead projector marker to each group. Tell students to place the sentence strips facedown.

7. Explain that students will take turns drawing a sentence from the pile. Each person will conduct the index finger test on the sentence he or she

draws. Have students add commas where needed with the overhead transparency marker.

8. When all groups are finished correcting the last sentence, show an overhead answer key and review the answers as a whole class.

9. Have students clean the strips with a wet paper towel and place them back in the envelopes.

Activity 7 Stomp Out Run-ons

Objective	To identify and correct run-ons in student writing
Time	Two 40-minute class periods
Materials	● 12" x 18" white construction paper (one piece per student)
	● colored markers ● crayons ● colored pencils ● rulers
	● one copy per student of the Rubric for Stomp Out Run-ons (page 79)

Step-by-Step

1. Provide the following list of directions for students before they begin the project:

   • Find and write down the run-ons labeled in the compositions in your writing folder.

   • Correct the run-ons using the three methods you have been taught.

   • On scrap paper, design a shoe or another piece of footwear. At the top of an 12" x 18" piece of construction paper neatly write the title *Stomp Out Run-ons*. Fill the remaining

   space with the final version of your shoe. Use a ruler to draw straight, evenly-spaced lines on the footwear. Write your corrected run-ons directly on the shoe. If you need more room, write around or below the shoe.

   • Use a dark marker or pen to write the sentences.

   • Color neatly.

   • Put your name, date, and section on the back of the shoe.

2. Have students design colorful footwear to demonstrate their knowledge of correcting run-ons.

3. Have students write several of their corrected run-ons on and around the shoe, slipper, or boot.

4. When all of the shoes are completed, use the Rubric for Stomp Out Run-ons to evaluate the footwear. Award prizes for Biggest Run-on, Most Humorous Shoe, Most Sophisticated, Most Colorful, Most Unique, Best Runner, Hippest Shoe, Busiest Shoe, and Most Creative Theme. Display the shoes on the bulletin board and in the hall.

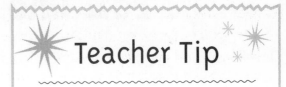

Teacher Tip

Before I teach the mini-lessons on run-ons, I bracket and label run-ons in my students' writing. Once students learn the three ways to repair run-ons —add a comma, add a semicolon, or add end punctuation—I have them correct all of the run-ons in their writing folders.

Foil the Fragments

Directions: Read the story below. Use brackets and this proofreading symbol to identify each fragment: (frag). Correct the fragments by (1) adding words, or (2) using the proper proofreading symbols to connect thoughts and make complete sentences.

The day started and ended. Like a living nightmare. When I awoke. Streams of sunlight poured through my window. My heart immediately. Went into overdrive. The alarm had not rung! Panicking, I eyeballed the clock. Which read 7:05 A.M. The bus arrived at 7:10. Frantic, I bolted out of bed. Brushed my teeth and whipped on some clothes. As I sprinted down the stairs. I tripped and sailed out the door. Heard my mother scream, "What about breakfast?"

Panting and breathless. I arrived at the bus stop just in time to board. When I stepped onto the bus. Everyone burst out laughing. My hair stood up like a porcupine's quills! Worse yet, I was wearing. My Winnie-the-Pooh pajama shirt! On my left foot a black leather loafer glistened. On my right foot a white, high-top sneaker!

With my pale face burning bright red. I squeezed into a seat next to the class clown. Who had planted a huge wad of prechewed grape bubble gum in my spot. As I stood up and tried to pull the goo off of me. I looked like an insect inside a spider's web. Strands of gum entangled me from head to toe. While I shrieked like an insane hyena. The bus driver called for help on his cell phone. When help arrived and put my gum-entwined body on a stretcher. I muttered, "Well, this sure beats homework."

Name: _____ Date: _____ Final Score: _____

Rubric for the Forget Fragments Puzzle

4—Advanced

Includes all required information: title, name, date, and section.

The fragment is properly corrected.

Sentences are very neatly written.

All mechanics are correct.

The puzzle pieces are neatly colored, eye-catching, and appealing.

3—Proficient

Includes most required information: title, name, date, and section.

The corrected fragment has minor sentence sense or structure problems.

Sentences are legible and are written in a straight line.

Most mechanics are correct.

The puzzle piece is neatly colored.

2—Basic

Includes some required information: title, name, date, and section.

The corrected fragment has major sentence sense or structure problems.

Sentences are not as neat as they should be.

There are some errors in mechanics.

The puzzle piece has little color.

1—Below Basic

Includes little or no required information: title, name, date, and section.

The fragment is not properly corrected.

Sentences are not neatly written.

There are many errors in mechanics.

The puzzle piece is not colored.

I have a pesky brother and a spoiled sister too but my brother is far more dangerous.

He put a dead worm on the pew at church and everyone stared at me when I shrieked.

Later the same day the brat stuck an anchovy inside my peanut butter sandwich but, of course, the little creep did not tell me.

I bit into the salty fish and started to choke, sputter, and cry.

That mischievous brother of mine pretended to feel sorry for me but I still suspected he was responsible for the dirty trick.

Next, he crumpled my math homework and drew paw prints all over it so my math teacher yelled at me in front of everyone.

I was steaming when I came home yet I pretended that I had had a great day.

Since my brother was at baseball practice, I short-sheeted the bed, filled it with peanuts, and stuffed the pillow with hay.

Then I drenched the sheets and my brother's p.j.'s in glue.

Later I heard screams and tons of wheezy sneezes for my fiendish brother was stuck to the peanuts and straw-filled pillow.

Name: _____ Date: _____ Final Score: _____

Rubric for Stomp Out Run-ons

4–Advanced

Includes all required information: title, name, date, and section.

The run-on(s) is/are properly corrected.

Sentences are very neatly written.

All mechanics are correct.

The footwear is neatly colored, eye-catching, and appealing.

3–Proficient

Includes most required information: title, name, date, and section.

The corrected run-on has minor sentence sense or structure problems.

Sentences are legible and are written in a straight line.

Most mechanics are correct.

The footwear is neatly colored.

2–Basic

Includes some required information: title, name, date, and section.

The corrected run-on has major sentence sense or structure problems.

Sentences are not as neat as they should be.

There are some errors in mechanics.

The footwear has little color.

1–Below Basic

Includes little or no required information: title, name, date, and section.

The run-on(s) is/are not properly corrected.

Sentences are not neatly written.

There are many errors in mechanics.

The footwear is not colored.

Bibliography

Armstrong, T. *Multiple Intelligences in the Classroom.* Alexandria, VA: American Association for Supervision and Curriculum Development, 1998.

Brandt, R. *Powerful Learning.* Alexandria, VA: American Association for Supervision and Curriculum Development, 1998.

Brink, S., "Smart Moves," *U.S. News and World Report*, May 15, 1995, 76–84.

Brooks, J.G. & M.G. Brooks. *In Search of Understanding: The Case for Constructivist Classrooms.* Alexandria, VA: American Association for Supervision and Curriculum Development, 1993.

Hannaford, C. "Smart Moves," *Learning*, no. 25, 3, November/December, 1996: 66–68.

Jensen, E. *Teaching With the Brain in Mind.* Alexandria, VA: American Association for Supervision and Curriculum Development, 1998.

Moss, S. & M. Fuller. "Implementing Effective Practices: Teachers' Perspective," *Phi Delta Kappan*, no. 82, 4, December, 2000: 273–276.

Nicholson–Nelson, K. *Developing Students' Multiple Intelligences.* New York: Scholastic Professional Books, 1998.

Silver, H., R. Strong & M. Perini. *So Each May Learn: Integrating Learning Styles and Multiple Intelligences.* Alexandria, VA: American Association for Supervision and Curriculum Development, 2000.

Sprenger, M. *Learning and Memory: The Brain in Action.* Alexandria, VA: American Association for Supervision and Curriculum Development, 1999.

Tomlinson, C.A. *How to Differentiate Instruction in Mixed-Ability Classrooms.* Alexandria, VA: American Association for Supervision and Curriculum Development, 1995.

Wolfe, P. *Brain Matters: Translating Research into Classroom Practice.* Alexandria, VA: American Association for Supervision and Curriculum Development, 2001.

Web Resources

The Web sites listed below either contain interactive lessons and games classroom teachers can use, or they provide engaging activities for students.

Daily Grammar	http://www.dailygrammar.com
English–Zone.com	http://www.english-zone.com
Grammar Bytes	http://www.chompchomp.com/exercises.htm
Guide to Grammar and Writing	http://www.webster.commnet.edu/grammar/nouns.htm
The Teacher's Desk	http://teachersdesk.org
Teachers.Net	http://www.teachers.net/lessons/
The Wide World of Verbs	http://www.kyrene.k12.az.us/schools/brisas/sunda/verb/enter.htm